ENGLAND

LEE THOMAS

Designed and Produced by

Ted Smart & David Gibbon

**CRESCENT BOOKS
NEW YORK**

So much has been written about England; there is no other country which has been so eulogised throughout the centuries; and yet Keats' gentle lyricism belies the patriotic passion that lies behind that lovely verse and encapsulates the fierce pride that dwells within the English breast.

This mongrel breed, which has so readily absorbed the cultures and languages of a good many foreign invaders, embellished them and made them its own, will stoutly defend the amorphous 'Englishness' of an Englishman – for to be English does not necessarily mean that one has to be of purebred English stock (indeed few are!) – it is rather a passion for the country itself: its *'green and pleasant land'*; the vagaries of the weather, and the sure belief that no other country on earth can be such a 'commodious' place in which to live.

It is not surprising that this tiny country reveals such a rich diversity of landscape, for although comparatively young on the geological time scale, its complex structure, spanning 600,000,000 years, illustrates almost every stage of geological history, from the oldest igneous rocks of the extreme west and north to the recent alluvial soils of reclaimed fenland in East Anglia. Some of the most splendid examples can be seen in the striking shoreline cliff structures, particularly those of the ancient granite precipices at Land's End, succeeding through the vari-coloured sandstones and multi-aged limestones to the dazzling white chalk bluffs of the South Downs, and the rugged desert sandstones of the northern Pennines, with their wild, bleak moors, that split the north of England longitudinally.

The earliest known human remains in Britain, dating back approximately a quarter of a million years, are the fragments of a human skull found in a gravel pit by the lower Thames at Swanscombe, and the Swanscombe Man, as he is now referred to, is recognised as one of the direct ancestors of Homo sapiens. By the time the North Sea had been formed (about 6,000 B.C.) and the mainland link with France severed, the island was populated by hunters who were also to become skilled in the arts of carpentry and fishing, and who were later joined by foreign immigrants, including a short, swarthy-complexioned Mediterranean people who settled in the Cotswolds and on the chalk hills, about 2,400 B.C. These New Stone Age farmers, the first in Britain, were responsible for the building of the long, narrow burial mounds, or barrows, predominantly conspicuous on the chalk downlands, and the megalithic tombs that were built by the settlers along the western coast.

By the end of the New Stone Age, Britain's most famous and awe-inspiring megalithic monument – Stonehenge – was under construction, with the completion of the outer circular ditch and bank, a ring of 56 pits known as the Aubrey Holes just inside the bank, and the Heel stone which stands 256 feet from the centre circle on the avenue leading from the north-eastern break in the bank. During the second millennium, about 1800 B.C., the Beaker Folk arrived from Holland and the Rhineland, at the dawn of the Bronze Age. They played a major role, not only in the second stage of development at Stonehenge with the transportation of the pillars of igneous rock or 'bluestones' from the

Prescelly Mountains in South-West Wales, but also in the creation of the fascinating Avebury Stone Circle – some one hundred sarsen stones of huge dimensions – which ring the picturesque Wiltshire Village. Stonehenge was later remodelled during the 15th century B.C. when about eighty huge blocks of sarsen were brought from the Marlborough Downs to form a unique circle, with its carefully shaped lintels and trilithons, and inner horseshoe formation, the remains of which can still be seen today.

From the brooding mystery of Stonehenge to the northern limit of Roman occupation – Hadrian's Wall – England has a wealth of fascinating history which is woven into the very fabric of its hills and dales, bustling towns and cities, sleepy villages and sea-washed shores and, in spite of the fact that over the centuries the landscape has been significantly changed by its occupants, the basic structure of life in scattered groups, whether in modern cities or close-knit villages, perpetuates the picture of England as a pastoral country that still persists even in the 20th century.

The South West: Cornwall and Devon

Rocky coastlines pounded by the spuming white foam of Atlantic breakers and a northern coast of soft, sandy beaches contrasted with the calmer waters of the South West's famed 'Riviera', where sparkling blue waters lap the tiny coves and bays that lie on its opposite shore, and, between, the wild, wind-blown moors, rolling hills and steep river valleys – South West England is steeped in centuries of romantic legend. It was amid this land of sudden mists that King Arthur and his Knights of the Round Table were said to have kept their court; it was this land that nurtured the Elizabethan sea-adventurers – Raleigh, Drake and Hawkins – whose tall-masted ships sailed the Spanish Main and the routes to the 'New World'; the land that inspired writers and poets, such as the novelist Daphne Du Maurier, who wove her story of romance and intrigue, 'Frenchman's Creek', around the spectacular scenery of its crenellated shoreline.

Until modern times Cornwall was virtually isolated from the rest of the country, the Tamar River forming a formidable barrier with neighbouring Devon as it slices across the peninsula from Woolley Barrow to the Plymouth Sound, until Brunel's elegant Victorian bridge at Saltash carried the railway across the river. This feeling of remoteness is nowhere better illustrated than in the lonely Longships Lighthouse, standing beyond the granite grandeur of Land's End, at the tip of the Penwith Peninsula, where countless ships have perished on the merciless rocks. The shoreline is peppered with picturesque fishing villages and yachting resorts, each with its own distinctive charm and mystery, that now play host to the vast numbers of tourists who flock, each summer, to spend their leisure time here.

From The Lizard, the southernmost part of England, with its soaring cliffs and pinnacles of rock reaching down to Lizard

Cottages at Lyndhurst in the New Forest, Hampshire left.

Point, up to Camborne, once the centre of Cornwall's tin mining industry, and beyond, the old pump houses, once so necessary to the miners to guard against the flooding with which they were constantly threatened, still dot the landscape. Cliff-top churches perch atop the craggy bluffs that overlook the sand and shingle beaches; cob and thatch cottages line the winding country lanes of Devon amid the rich, red-soiled farming land, and slate and granite cots hug the inland, windswept moors. Stirring reminders of past history, such as Pendennis Castle at Falmouth; Restormel Castle, close to Lostwithiel; the Methodist 'Cathedral' at Gwennap Pit, where John Wesley preached in the mid-18th century and St Michael's Mount, opposite Penzance, which, according to legend, is part of the lost kingdom of Lyonesse, where King Arthur's knights once rode, kindle the imagination, while the bleak and wild moors of Bodmin and Dartmoor are renowned for their rugged, isolated beauty.

Cornwall's cathedral city and administrative centre is Truro, noted for its striking, triple-tiered cathedral which was completed in 1910. For eight centuries the Sees of Cornwall and Devon were united, until the reconstitution of the Cornish See in 1897.

Exeter, in Devon, the South West's major city, and one of England's most historic, contains the remains of one of the largest Roman bath houses ever to be excavated in Britain, as well as a magnificent 14th-century cathedral (thought to be its crowning glory) noted for its two outstanding Norman towers and renowned carved figures on the West Front; plus a wealth of fine buildings, mansions, castles and abbeys.

It was from Plymouth, the largest city in the West Country, that the Pilgrim Fathers, aboard the Mayflower, set sail for America in 1620. Here, over three centuries later, in 1966, the city would witness the start of another epic journey, that of Sir Francis Chichester's, as he commenced his successful single-handed voyage around the world.

One of the South West's show-pieces is undoubtedly picturesque Clovelly, lying in a lush, narrow combe between the steep Devon cliffs. Cars are banned from the village and the precipitous main street is almost continually filled with fragrant, colourful flowers. East of sophisticated Torquay, Devon's largest and most famous seaside resort, is spectacular Kent's Cavern, occupied by prehistoric men and animals during the last Ice-Age, and one of the oldest known human dwelling-places in Britain.

It is not surprising that this beautiful region of England, occupied from Neolithic times through the Roman invasion, and a bastion of the old Celtic ways, should continue to beckon the artists and writers for whom it has long provided ideal inspiration, as well as the scores of holiday-makers, who at the end of their stay are loathe to forsake its charms, for its diversity of landscape, blessed with the country's mildest climate, affords a distinctive variety of scenery within a compact area, that marks the peculiar mystique of England.

Southern Counties: Somerset, Wiltshire, Dorset, Hampshire, Isle of Wight

*'On either side the river lie
Long fields of barley and of rye,
That clothe the wold and meet the sky,
And thro' the field the road runs by
To many-tower'd Camelot'*

'The Lady of Shalott' *Alfred, Lord Tennyson*

A great profusion of well-blended beauty and quiet solitude amid pastoral landscapes rich in historic remains, from the neolithic monuments on Salisbury Plain to the elegant Georgian architecture of Bath, clothes the rural loveliness of the Southern Counties.

Surrounded by myth and legend, Glastonbury in Somerset, lying on slopes that incline from the Brue Valley to a 522 ft tor, topped by the fragmented remains of the Benedictine abbey of St Mary, is the cradle of Christianity in Britain. It is said that when Joseph of Arimathea came to the town, bringing with him the chalice used at the Last Supper, he leant in prayer on his thorn staff, which immediately took root, indicating that he should stay and found a religious house. The winter-flowering Glastonbury thorn-tree that sprang from the original root on Wirrall Hill is purported to have been hacked down by a Roundhead during the Civil War, but a thorn-tree in the abbey grounds is claimed to be a cutting from it. According to Arthurian legend, King Arthur, whose Camelot is thought to be Cadbury Castle, near Sutton Mentis, and his Queen, Guinevere, were re-interred in the abbey, and the Holy Grail, brought by Joseph, which Arthur's knights sought, is believed to be buried below the Chalice Spring on Glastonbury Tor.

Considered to be the loveliest part of Somerset, the undulating, wooded Quantock Hills have close affiliations with the poets Coleridge and Wordsworth, who strolled amid the dark, tangled woods and heather-covered moorland, whilst Blackmore's evocative 'Lorna Doone' conjures images of the lonely Mendip Hills, rent by the towering limestone cliffs of the awe-inspiring Cheddar Gorge.

Facing the Severn estuary and the southern part of the Cotswolds Hills, the county of Avon contains the spectacular Avon Gorge, spanned by Brunel's remarkable Clifton Suspension Bridge towering 245 ft above the Avon River's high-water level and affording some of the finest panoramic views of the gorge and surrounding countryside. Bristol, combining old and new in pleasing proportions, has been a thriving commercial port since the 10th century. It was from this important city that John Cabot set sail in discovery of North America and Newfoundland, in 1497, in the 100-ton *Matthew;* and in 1552 was founded the Society of Merchant Venturers who played such an important role in the development of the mighty Empire.

Around the Roman baths of the settlement of Aquae Sulis, chosen for the valuable mineral waters that originate in the Eastern Mendips, grew the beautiful city that was to take their name and which was to come to the full flowering of its grace and charm during Georgian times. Although prosperous throughout the Middle Ages, Bath's fame is closely associated with the high society of the Regency period, when the talented dandy, Beau Nash, presided over the pump-room balls and elegant assemblies, so delightfully described in Jane Austen's 19th-century novels.

As famous as the prehistoric monuments that rise from the vast stillness of Wiltshire's Salisbury Plain, New Sarum, or Salisbury, built at the confluence of four river valleys, and one of the loveliest of England's many cathedral cities, is famed for its magnificent centrepiece, set amid a splendid conglomeration of varying architectural styles – the resplendent mediaeval cathedral with its majestic, soaring spire and graceful cloisters, eulogised by Trollope. Among its many treasures is one of the four original copies of Magna Carta which is housed in the library over the East Walk. West of the city lie the valleys of the Wylye and the Nadder, divided by the forest downlands of Grovely Wood and the Great Ridge, along which can be traced the route of a Roman road as it swings west towards Bath.

Dorset is rich farming country, famous for its rolling pastures providing its creamy milk and delicious cheeses. Immortalised by the great English novelist and observer of rural life, Thomas Hardy, who was born in the picturesque hamlet of Bockhampton, the pastoral scenes provided memorable backgrounds to many of his famous novels. Belying the undisturbed, rural tranquillity, however, is a dramatic coastline, particularly impressive in the crumbling, limestone cliffs which culminate in Durdle Door, a massive, natural arch of Purbeck stone that guards the entrance to Man O' War Bay.

England, as a maritime nation, has always had strong associations with the sea. Nowhere is this more evident than along the coast of Hampshire; Buckler's Hard may seem an unlikely setting today, with horses grazing on the wide, main street, but it was here, in the 18th century, that many of the ships were built which were to sail under the command of Nelson in the Napoleonic War. This naval tradition is carried on, and brought up to date, at Portsmouth, with its great dockyards and training schools, and a poignant reminder of its past is Nelson's flagship, the *Victory*, berthed among sheds of red brick and concrete in the dockyard itself, on board which this most famous of England's naval heroes died.

Synonymous with Hampshire is the New Forest – the famed royal hunting ground which was a favourite of King John – its vast woodland teeming with a variety of wildlife including the celebrated New Forest pony. Today this oldest of the great forests of England, covering 145 square miles, is administered by a special group of officials, called Verderers, who are responsible for maintaining law and order, in addition to the welfare of the many animals which inhabit the preserve.

Separated from the Hampshire coastline, with its wealth of fine resorts, by the Solent and Spithead, lies the delightful holiday island of the Isle of Wight, a favourite of the Victorians since Queen Victoria endorsed its qualities. It was in the royal country retreat of Osborne House in East Cowes, that Queen Victoria died in 1901.

South-East England: East and West Sussex, Surrey and Kent

> *'Meadows trim with daisies pied,*
> *Shallow brooks and rivers wide*
> *Towers, and battlements it sees*
> *Bosom'd high in tufted trees,*
> *Where perhaps some beauty lies,*
> *The cynosure of neighbouring eyes.'*
> 'Lycidas' *John Milton*

Trim meadows and wide-ribboned rivers are woven into the texture of this prominent corner of England as it juts boldly into the English Channel, whilst its gleaming, white chalk cliffs are backed by the rolling Sussex Downs, littered with a host of ruined fortifications that bear witness to successive armies of invaders who, throughout the centuries, have left their marks on this, their first foothold on the land they set out to conquer.

The Romans succeeded in subjugating the country to their laws for a while, but then abandoned it and went back to their homeland. William and his Normans, as every schoolboy knows,

landed at, or near, Hastings, then made their way inland to Battle to face a weary army. Tricked by the Normans into believing that they were retreating, the Saxons chased them in disarray and paid dearly for their mistake. Their king was dead and the country had a new ruler. The last successful invasion of England had become history! Whenever defences are breached they tend to be strengthened by the conquerors, to ensure that they cannot be caught out by others intent on following their example and this, largely, accounts for the great wealth of castles around the coast, such as the particularly fine examples at Arundel and Bodiam.

Sussex is by no means only a county of historic castles and battlefields, however. The South Downs are full of natural beauty, and wooded hills and valleys, delightful villages and fine coastal resorts are part of the area's enormous variety. The picturesque old town of Rye, once a lively port, but now left stranded by the receding sea, still retains the character it had when it was a notorious haunt of smugglers. Eastbourne, at one time a small fishing village, is still the elegant resort that the 7th Duke of Devonshire designed in 1834, and nearby Beachy Head, the highest cliff on the south coast, towering 534 ft above the sea, still attracts countless visitors who can, on a clear day, glimpse the Isle of Wight to the west and Dungeness to the east. Brighton, possibly the most well-known resort on the Sussex coast, with its fairy-tale Royal Pavilion, is an intriguing confection of graceful Georgian houses, gaudy sea-side paraphernalia, bracing sea-air and delightful old shops and houses that line the narrow, picturesque 'Lanes'. Just west of the cathedral town of Chichester lies one of the major Roman relics in Britain, at Fishbourne, where excavations have revealed an important Roman palace occupied during the 2nd and 3rd centuries A.D., while south-east of the Black Down, the highest point in Sussex, stands the mediaeval town of Petworth and the magnificent mansion of Petworth House, with its superb art collection that includes a series of exquisite Turner paintings of the local landscapes that the artist loved so well.

Although to many people Surrey conjures up the image of one vast London commuter land, the county has, nevertheless, managed to retain much of its natural beauty in generous open spaces, such as Box Hill, one of the South East's best known beauty spots on the North Downs and a popular picnic area as long ago as the reign of Charles II, and in its charming villages, rich in historic interest. The very banks of the River Thames, as it winds its way through the countryside, endorse the fact. Runnymede saw the granting by King John of the draft of Magna Carta in 1215 and the site now stands in National Trust Property. Historic Richmond, so named by Henry VII to commemorate his original title of Duke of Richmond, stands on the slopes of a hill from the top of which may be seen a famous and most beautiful view of the river. Nearby Kingston-upon-Thames has been a royal borough for over 1,100 years. Outside the Guildhall may be seen the 'King's Stone' on which several Saxon Kings are said to have been crowned. The county also contains some of the country's finest botanical gardens: Kew Gardens which was landscaped by 'Capability' Brown, with its great Palm House and whimsical Pagoda; the Royal Horticultural Society's delightful 300-acre experimental gardens at Wisley, and Winkworth Arboretum's superb woodland acres.

Often referred to as 'the garden of England', the fertile soil of Kent has supported orchards and vineyards since Roman times. Hops, too, have been grown in the county for over four thousand years and today the hop fields cover some 10,000 acres, mainly in the Medway Valley and in a belt from Faversham to Canterbury, where traditional, conical-roofed oast-houses for hop drying are a familiar and pretty part of the rural scene. Beyond the rich valleys the North Downs stretch towards the Kent coastline, peppered with myriad coastal ports that once presented the first line of defence against invaders, culminating in the famed white cliffs of Dover as they preside over the narrowest part of the English Channel. For centuries Dover has played a major role in British history, and the road, from this busiest of English passenger ports, to Canterbury — the birthplace of Christianity in Saxon England, to where mediaeval pilgrims trudged the ancient trackway of the 'Pilgrims Way', so eloquently represented by Chaucer, that they might worship at the shrine of the murdered Thomas à Becket in the long, grey cathedral that dominates the city and which is the Mother Church of Anglicans throughout the world – still follows the route of the Roman Watling Street.

London

'Earth has not anything to show more fair:
Dull would he be of soul who could pass by
A sight so touching in its majesty…
The river glideth at his own sweet will…
And all that mighty heart is lying still!'

'Upon Westminster Bridge' *William Wordsworth*

How to describe this truly magnificent city that can be almost all things to all men, and about which countless words have already been written? Ever growing, its very size can be daunting – its contemporary boundaries encompassing a collection of villages, hamlets and even 'new towns' which have, in comparatively recent times, been swallowed up to become part of the vast conglomeration of Greater London. Called by the Romans Londinium and defined by city walls which still contain the city proper, it has been added to throughout the centuries to leave a legacy of fine buildings, streets and squares that fan out from the mighty Thames – the broad-ribboned river to which the city owes much of its importance. Architectural gems of the past – St Paul's Cathedral, the Tower, Westminster Abbey, Big Ben – the list is endless – all jostle for space amid the newer additions; for example the gleaming high-rise buildings and now-familiar landmark of the Post Office Tower. Yet, as though to balance this wealth of stone, London contains an abundance of parks, gardens and open spaces – the 'green fields of London' – in which to walk along fragrant pathways or sit beside tranquil lakes, is to forget that sometimes only yards away the silence is broken by the noisy hum of a mighty city hurrying by. All the best that can be offered in any city throughout the world can be found here – art galleries and museums, churches and mansions, internationally-known stores and restaurants, and, of course, the country's unique pomp and pageantry that is symbolic of a monarchy which has stood at the nation's helm since time immemorial.

The Home Counties: Berkshire, Oxfordshire, Buckinghamshire, Bedfordshire, Hertfordshire

'Moor'd to the cool bank in the
summer heats, Mid wide grass meadows
which the sunshine fills,
And watch the warm, green-muffled
Cumner hills, And wonder if thou
haunt'st their shy retreats.'

'The Scholar Gypsy' *Matthew Arnold*

Fanning westwards and north of London, the rich diversity of landscape that marks the five 'Home Counties' of England is due, primarily, to the three hill regions of the Chilterns, the Cotswolds and the Berkshire Downs, and the meandering rivers, notably the Thames and the Great Ouse, that wind through this fascinating area suffused in ancient history.

From its source in the Cotswolds the orderly Thames flows through Oxfordshire and Berkshire, its lush water-meadows marking the counties' boundary. To the south of the river, on the bold escarpment of the Berkshire Downs bordering the fertile, flat farmlands, looms the 374 ft figure of the White Horse, after which the Vale is named. Myth and controversy surround this gigantic form which, some claim, was cut into the chalk in Saxon times, while others assert that the art-style is similar to that of the Iron Age Celts and believe that the figure is representative of their goddess Epona, protectress of horses. The ancient tracks of the Icknield Way and Ridge Way, as they cross the lovely Berkshire Downs, also give some indication of how far back in antiquity people have occupied the area. Although the county is punctuated with a wealth of historic mansions, the most celebrated is undoubtedly that of Windsor Castle as it dominates the leafy banks of the glorious Thames. Built by William the Conqueror, and improved and embellished by succeeding monarchs, the castle first became a royal home during the reign of Henry I. Contained within its soft grey walls is some of the finest architecture in England, notably in the magnificent St George's Chapel.

Where the Thames meets the Cherwell, in the Upper Thames Basin, and is known as the Isis, rise the honey-coloured stone buildings and 'dreaming spires' of Oxfordshire's crowning glory and its ancient seat of learning – Oxford – part of England's cultural heritage. It was during the 8th century that the city was formed with the founding of St Frideswide's nunnery. By 1214 a university was established and before the close of the 13th century the four colleges of Balliol, Merton, St Edmund Hall and University had been instituted. Over the succeeding centuries other historic colleges swelled their ranks, to where those with propensity would seek the dissemination of knowledge, within those hallowed walls.

Dramatically rent by the low chalk ridge of the Chilterns, the face of Buckinghamshire presents one of England's richest agricultural regions, Creslow Great Field, on its northern profile, and a countryside of beechwoods and bluebells, mossy banks and silver streams on its southern. It was in this county, so full of history, in an old stone church surrounded by a huge, gilded ball, which perches on a hilltop in West Wycombe Park, that the members of the notorious Hell Fire Club, an 18th-century group of gamblers and rakes, met to plot their witchcraft orgies. At Jordan, near Beaconsfield, can be seen beams that formed part of the Pilgrim Father's 'Mayflower'; Penn was the home of William Penn, the founder of Pennsylvania in the 'New World', and in

Chalfont St Giles stands the mellow cottage which was inhabited by Milton when he fled London to escape the Great Plague in 1665. Oddly enough, Buckingham is not the county seat, although it once was. It was given the title by Alfred the Great, but lost it in 1725, when the honour was transferred to Aylesbury. The county of Buckinghamshire reflects so admirably the fascination of English history in that it is made up of so many small incidents, as well as the great and the obvious.

From Buckinghamshire the Great Ouse curves its way through the green pasturelands of north Bedfordshire, a peaceful region that has remained unspoilt by the passage of time. Straddling the great river is the county town of Bedford, with its attractive conglomerate of varying architectural styles, closely associated with John Bunyan – of 'The Pilgrim's Progress' fame – who spent over half his life in the town (although a great deal of it in Bedford Jail!). This beautiful county displays its most varied scenery in its southernmost tip, where the windblown Dunstable Downs, affording views over nine counties, provide an ideal launching ground for gliders. High on the Downs is sited the unique and internationally-known zoo of Whipsnade, where visitors do not even need to step out of their cars to see many of the animals! Here, too, is the magnificent stately home of Woburn, with its famous Wildlife Park.

Picturesque Hertfordshire, although bisected by arterial roads since Roman times, is one of the country's prettiest counties. Leafy lanes wind and loop through the grassy hills and steep little valleys of the rural countryside, where half-timbered houses and thatched-roofed cottages huddle in numerous scattered villages. Hertfordshire, too, has its rich share of history. The city of St Albans dates back 2,000 years, and is the third important town on the site. Its magnificent abbey, originally built by the Saxons to commemorate Britain's first Christian martyr, St Alban, was rebuilt by the Normans and later enlarged, in the 13th century. West of the city stands the splendid, ruined remains of Verulamium, one of the finest Roman towns in England, exhibiting a fine example of a huge theatre which dates from the mid-2nd century A.D., in addition to important remains that are housed in a nearby museum. It was in the Old Palace, adjoining the splendid Jacobean mansion of Hatfield House, that Queen Elizabeth I spent much of her childhood, while the impressive grounds of Knebworth House, the family home of the Lyttons, have in recent years, become famous as the annual venue of internationally-known 'pop star' concerts.

Eastern Counties: Essex, Suffolk, Norfolk, Cambridgeshire

'Now fades the glimmering landscape
on the sight, And all the air
a solemn stillness holds,
Save where the beetle wheels
his droning flight,
And drowsy tinklings lull
the distant folds.'
'Elegy in a Country Churchyard' *Thomas Gray*

The rump of England astride the Wash, its patchwork farmlands forming an autumnal-hued counterpane across the landscape, has for centuries accommodated numerous invaders who swept in from the sea. Its spacious pasturelands, unforgettably captured on canvas by the great artist Constable, have close associations with some of England's most influential names: it was the land that Boudicca ruled; the birthplace of Oliver Cromwell, Thomas Clarkson and Elizabeth Fry, while through the halls of its beautiful university – Cambridge – have passed a succession of writers who have left an indelible mark on English literature.

Essex is a county of immense contrasts, from the great forested acres of Epping that border the sprawling metropolis of Greater London, through the bustle of industry of the Thames-side area where the bright lights of Southend-on-Sea beckon Londoners to their favourite seaside resort, to the coastal belt of reclaimed marshland that stretches from Shoeburyness to the Blackwater Estuary and includes Foulness, the largest island in the Thames Estuary; its lonely territory playing host, during the winter months, to an estimated 10,000 Brent Geese after they have flown south from their Arctic breeding grounds. The mudflats and winding creeks, with which this part of the coast abounds, has provided ideal conditions for the oysters that are produced here, and the ancient city of Colchester, the heart of the trade, traditionally holds an annual oyster feast that is quite unique.

Along the crumbling coastline of Suffolk stands Dunwich, one of the most evocative of East Anglia's villages – once the Roman town of Sitomagus and a prosperous trading port with France – which has now largely vanished below the sea. Although little is left of this once-thriving town, devastated by a storm in the 14th century, the sight of its ruined priory and desolate shingle beach beneath the still eroding cliffs fosters an unaccountable emotional experience that is quite uncanny. Numerous writers and artists, including Edward FitzGerald, the translator of 'The Rubáiyát of Omar Khayyám', drew inspiration amid its tragic haunts. It is in the churchyard at Boulge, in the open farmlands of central Suffolk, that FitzGerald lies buried – beneath scented roses that flower from a seed of a tree on the grave of Omar Khayyám and sent from Naishapur. For most people it would be impossible to divorce the Suffolk that we see today from the county that John Constable painted and which was his home. He was born in the village of East Bergholt and spent much of his life in painting the countryside which he knew and loved. The River Stour and its locks and banks were especial favourites with him and formed the subjects of many of his best loved works. Possibly the best known, and certainly the one most visited by tourists, is Willy Lott's Cottage at Flatford Mill. Carefully preserved, it remains almost unchanged to this day and looks very much as it must have done to the artist when he sat down by the water with his canvas and brushes.

Norfolk is synonymous with 'The Broads', some 200 miles of open expanses of water with navigable approach channels which, linked with lakes, rivers and waterways – some manmade – make up this delightful area that is seen to advantage from one of the many boats on hire to tourists. Because of the flat, open landscape in this part of the country, wind-driven mills were, for many years, used to grind corn, and it is estimated that there were about one thousand five hundred such mills at work until a century ago. Although their numbers have dwindled since then, enough remain still to form a picturesque part of the rural landscape. The magnificent cathedral of Holy Trinity in Norwich is the only remaining example in England that conforms to the Apsidal plan, with the Bishop's throne behind the altar, a relic of the days in the early history of Christianity when Roman basilicas were used in the practice of the new religion. While Norwich undoubtedly exhibits a wealth of historic interest, its outskirts too have their charms: Caistor St Edmund, for example, four miles south of the cathedral city, so legend asserts, once formed part of Boudicca's capital.

Hereward the Wake is a legendary figure in English history. A Saxon noble at the time of the occupation of England by William the Conqueror, he resolved to continue the fight against the Normans, and was successful in this for a considerable time – greatly aided by the fact that he took refuge, with his followers, in the Fen country, on the Isle of Ely. The area was almost inaccessible, consisting largely of treacherous marshes, and it is doubtful if any army could ever have reached him, had he not been betrayed by monks. Throughout the centuries that followed work was carried out on the draining of the Fens, but it was not until the 18th century that the Isle of Ely ceased to be an island. Dominating those vast, hedgeless fields is the mediaeval triumph of Ely Cathedral, its unique and magnificent octagonal lantern one of the finest engineering feats of the Middle Ages.

Gentle, undulating hills and peaceful valleys give Cambridgeshire a feeling of space and tranquillity which also permeates its lovely university city of Cambridge. It is a city that requires time spent in exploration to fully appreciate its rare beauty and fascination. The Bridge of Sighs, built in the style of the famous bridge of the same name in Venice, seems not at all out of place in this very English of cities, where punts, instead of gondolas, glide peacefully along the waters of the river that it spans. Renowned colleges, charming churches, quaint little bookshops, and the broad, sweeping lawns of the Backs, are among the many delights that the city has to offer. Perhaps of all the county's most famous literary figures, the name of Rupert Brooke first springs to mind. His poignant 'War Sonnets' earned him fame and popularity during the First World War, and it was to his home in the 'Old Vicarage' at Grantchester, where the poet first lived after leaving King's College, that Brooke dedicated his nostalgic poem, composed in 1912, in a café in Berlin, which epitomises the heartache experienced by many English exiles, particularly during periods of war.

South Midlands: Gloucestershire, Herefordshire and Worcestershire, Midlands, Warwickshire, Northamptonshire, Leicestershire.

'...And in her harmony of varied greens,
Woods, meadows, hedge-rows,
cornfields, all around
Much beauty intervenes,
Filling with harmony the ear and eye;
While o'er the mingling scenes
Far spreads the laughing sky'.

'Summer Images' *John Clare*

The 'Cockpit of England' is a term often used to describe the South Midlands, at the heart of the country, where a mediaeval cross on the village green at Meriden is said to mark the exact centre of England. This area was witness to a host of battles that more than once shaped the country's destiny, including those of the 'Wars of the Roses' and the dramatic clashes of the Civil War; giving rise to a long list of place names and dates, which history

students up and down the country could arguably claim are as agonising to them as they were to the combatants of the field!

Gloucestershire is inevitably linked with the Cotswold Hills that dominate its eastern half, while the mighty Severn River in the west effectively cut the county into two parts for many years, until the opening of the magnificent new suspension bridge, in 1966, gave greater accessibility to the voluptuous Forest of Dean, clothed with the delicious green mantle of an estimated 20 million trees. At the heart of the Severn Valley lies Gloucester, a rich agricultural centre in Roman times: its majestic cathedral containing the second largest mediaeval stained-glass window in the country.

To the west of the Malvern Hills and the lush orchards and market gardens of Worcestershire's Vale of Evesham, lies richly wooded Herefordshire, famed for its apples (accounting for over half of the country's cider production) as well as the white-faced breed of cattle which have been used all over the world to improve other breeds; its historic cathedral city, once the Saxon capital of West Mercia, straddling the meandering Wye River. Even before the Norman conquest Herefordshire, a prime target on the Welsh border, was defended by stout castles against raiders from the Black Mountains which flank the west of the county, and on scenic Symonds Yat can be seen the remains of one of those strongholds, that of Goodrich Castle, which eventually fell to the troops of Oliver Cromwell during the Civil War.

It is hard to believe that the sprawling and highly industrialised conurbation of Birmingham – Britain's second largest city with a population well in excess of one million – at the heart of the Midland plain, was, in Shakespeare's day, a thriving market town surrounded by open fields, with the Forest of Arden, north and west of the Avon River, covering some 200 square miles with leafy greenery. Yet not far from the city a wealth of picturesque villages and historic houses nestle amid the undulating countryside. Between Birmingham and Coventry, an important city since the 14th century, and famed for its controversial cathedral that was designed by Sir Basil Spence and consecrated in 1962, as well as its mediaeval 'suffragette' Lady Godiva (the wife of Leofric, Earl of Mercia) who is reputed to have ridden naked through its streets in protest at the oppression of its inhabitants, stands the village of Meriden with its famous cross. Here too, is Packwood House with its remarkable 17th-century garden of shaped yew trees symbolising the Sermon on the Mount; Compton Wynyates, one of the most beautiful Tudor houses in England, and the site of the first major battle of the Civil War, in 1642, at high-ridged Edge Hill. South of Coventry the mediaeval fortress of Warwick Castle dominates the wide-ribboned Avon as it flows gently through the pastoral landscape that has changed little since Warwickshire's famous bard inhabited the old market town of Stratford-upon-Avon. This famous birthplace of William Shakespeare, with its half-timbered black and white houses and red-brick Royal Shakespeare Theatre, has become one of the world's most famous tourist attractions, and from the poet's birthplace, the early-16th-century building in Henley Street, to his tomb in Holy Trinity Church, the fascination of the beautiful old town and its close affiliations with its son of genius can never fail to beguile and enrich each visitor.

Drained to the Wash by the Welland and the Nene rivers, the fertile soil of the famous foxhunting county of Northamptonshire patterns the northern section of its agricultural landscape with a quilting of rich, arable fields. Its bustling county town on the Nene has long been noted for its shoe industry – confirmed by the fact that it was responsible for the supply of some 1,500 shoes for

Cromwell's Roundheads during the Civil War. Charles II, however, was less than pleased with Northampton's compliance to fill the order, and wreaked his revenge in the destruction of its castle and town walls.

Like its neighbouring county, Leicestershire is primarily agricultural, with the emphasis on dairy farming: the delicious blue-veined Stilton cheese being produced near Melton Mowbray, the world-famous home of pork pies and the Quorn Hunt. It was here on the county's productive plains, at Bosworth Field, that the long-fought duels of the Wars of the Roses finally came to an end, when Henry of Lancaster was proclaimed Henry VII on the death of his adversary, the ill-fated Richard III, of the House of York. At the hub of the county town of Leicester, which boasts a modern university and a history dating back over 2,000 years, rises a Victorian, Gothic-inspired clock tower that pays tribute to four of the city's notable benefactors. The most famous of these was the powerful baron, Simon de Montfort, First Earl of Leicester, whose rebellion against the tyranny of his brother-in-law, Henry III, led to the establishment of the first English Parliament, in 1265. North-west of the city, beyond the once thickly-wooded slopes of Charnwood Forest, where, in ancient times, Bronze-Age men trod the craggy hills of Beacon Hill, stands Ashby-de-la-Zouch and its impressive ruined castle. Built in the 15th century by the First Lord Hastings, the castle was visited by many famous royal names, including Mary Queen of Scots, who twice stayed, as a most reluctant guest, in the custody of Lord Hasting's grandson, the First Earl of Huntingdon.

North Midlands: Salop, Staffordshire, Derbyshire, Nottinghamshire, Lincolnshire

'... There blow a thousand gentle airs,
And each a different perfume bears,
As if the loveliest plants and trees
Had vassal breezes of their own
To watch and wait on them alone...'

'The Golden Hour' (from 'Lalla Rookh') *Thomas Moore.*

It is true that two centuries of industrial growth have inevitably left scars on the North Midlands horizon, yet to picture this area, which runs from the borders of Wales in the west to the North Sea-washed coastline in the east, as one vast, grimy, manufacturing community, would be quite erroneous. The five counties within its borders encompass an enormous diversity of scenery, from the scattered orchards of Salop, through the verdant woodlands of Sherwood Forest, to the notched stone crests of Derbyshire's Peak District, whilst its roll-call of famous literary figures is firmly planted amid the ranks of those who have greatly contributed to the nation's cultural heritage.

South of the Severn River, the rich, sheep-farming country on the edge of the Clun Forest, dominated by the limestone ridge of Wenlock Edge, which was immortalised by A. E. Housman in 'A Shropshire Lad', is contrasted with the wild heathlands and wind-swept moors that mark the Welsh border, in Salop's fascinating south-west corner. Here stand the relics of fortified strongholds that were built to defend against Celtic marauders – one of the most romantic being the abandoned, 11th-century sandstone castle of Ludlow, its crenellated towers perched high above the tranquil Teme River – as well as a wealth of well-preserved manor houses and clustered villages sporting their distinctive black and white, box-framed houses. North of the Long Mynd, a ten mile stretch of bleak hills that crest a vast acreage of heath and moorland that is peppered by prehistoric defence earthworks and barrows, sits beautiful Shrewsbury, the county town, idyllically situated in a loop of the Severn. The surrounding countryside is punctured by patches of hill country that includes the dramatic rock mass of the Wrekin, where a beacon once burned in warning of the coming of the Spanish Armada. During the 18th century Salop became the greatest iron-producing area in England; the town of Ironbridge, perched on the slopes of the steep and narrow gorge swept by the Severn River, gaining fame when Abraham Darby constructed the world's first cast-iron bridge, in 1779. Today the 200-ft bridge, cast in the designer's foundry at Coalbrookdale, is restricted to pedestrians.

Fine glazed china decorated with a spectrum of rainbow colours and gaily patterned earthenware; exquisitely moulded figurines and exotic vases; these are just some of the wares of 'The Potteries', the north Staffordshire region that has become famous throughout the world for its handsome artifacts and which is inextricably linked with the most noted porcelain and pottery manufacturing names of Wedgwood, Spode, Copeland and Minton. Centred around Stoke-on-Trent, the city was formed in the early part of the 20th century by the amalgamation of the five towns of Burslem, Hanley, Longton, Stoke and Tunstall, which featured prominently in the memorable novels of Arnold Bennett, and a sixth town, Fenton. It was over two centuries ago that Josiah Wedgwood brought lasting fame to the area, aided by the creative genius of his designer John Flaxman, although the industry is known to have existed long before the Roman occupation. Away from the busy areas of commerce, however, Staffordshire too has its great share of natural beauty, one of the most outstanding features being glorious Cannock Chase, an oasis of heath and forest land that once formed a vast hunting ground for Plantagenet kings, which lies on the verge of south Staffordshire's Black Country.

Derbyshire's Peak District, with its lush valleys and cascading streams, winding rivers and tree-studded hills, great rocky crags and gentle undulating pastures, has been compared to the countryside of Switzerland, and has a scenic splendour that would be difficult to surpass anywhere in the world. It came as no surprise, therefore, when in 1951 over five hundred square miles of the county were designated an area of outstanding beauty and became Britain's first National Park. As might be expected in such a lovely setting, great country houses were built here by famous families. South of the town of Bakewell, famed as the home of the delicious Bakewell tarts, lies the turreted, mediaeval outline of Haddon Hall, a romantic old house surrounded by terraced gardens. Not far away, and in contrast to its almost rambling beauty, stands one of the truly great stately homes of England, the majestic classical mansion of Chatsworth House, set amid exquisite landscaped grounds, and built for the first Duke of Devonshire in the early 18th century.

While part of Nottinghamshire's face undeniably reveals the scars of industrialisation, notably in the collieries and their attendant slag heaps across the north-west coalfield belt, so vividly portrayed in the works of D. H. Lawrence, its boundaries encompass not only the 200,000 acres of flat agricultural land of the Isle of Axholme which was drained by the Dutchman, Cornelius Vermuyden in the 17th century, but also the green woodlands of romantic Sherwood Forest, the home of England's most popular folk hero, the elusive Robin Hood. It is true that the famous outlaw is identified with no less than ten other counties in the country and that Barnsdale Forest in Yorkshire has an equal claim to be called his home, yet somehow the remnants of the once-vast Sherwood Forest seem richer in association with the man whom tradition asserts is more fact than fiction.

The ferry from Hull in Humberside makes its way across the River Humber to New Holland in Lincolnshire. The area has more in common with the low-lying country of Holland than just a name, for it too is just about at sea level, and in springtime the fields are alive with the colours of the tulips that are grown in the rich soil of this part of the country. Yet not all the lands of Lincolnshire are flat and low-lying, by any means. There are also the rolling uplands of the Wolds, thick with sheep grazing on the pastures, and abundant in the wheat for which the area is so famous. In this countryside of hills and valleys may be found many charming villages and towns, including the birthplace of Alfred, Lord Tennyson, in Somersby. Of the county's many churches, abbeys, stately homes and other fine buildings, two stand out in particular, though for different reasons. The first is in the ancient town of Boston, on the River Witham and is known by the peculiar name of 'The Boston Stump'. It is, in fact, the tower of St Botolph's Church and is a landmark for many miles. The second is, not surprisingly, the magnificent cathedral that dominates the city of Lincoln which contains, in the Angel Choir, the finest decorated work to be found in the country.

The North West:
Cheshire, Merseyside, Lancashire, Isle of Man, Greater Manchester, Cumbria

'All things that love the sun
are out of doors;
The sky rejoices in the morning's birth;
The grass is bright with rain-drops;
on the moors
The Hare is running races
in her mirth;...'

'Resolution and Independence' *William Wordsworth*

Ranged along the convoluted coastline that overlooks the Irish Sea, with its back against the spiny Pennine Mountain Chain, the North West counties present not only a rich diversity of landscape that encompasses the celebrated Lakeland scenery of Cumbria, and the park-like countryside of the Cheshire Plain, but also a striking difference in character and accent that has persisted throughout the centuries.

Grassy banks of yellow-headed buttercups; wooded hilltops bearing traces of long-ago Roman occupation; gentle rivers curving through fertile farmland; picturesque towns with their distinctive 'magpie' houses, and timbered manors, beautifully illustrated in the 15th-century building of Bramall Hall and 16th-century Little Moreton Hall, are part of the immense, individual charm of Cheshire. It was at Knutsford that Mrs. Gaskell drew inspiration for her charming novel, 'Cranford', although the sight of the giant radio telescope of Jodrell Bank, standing like some science fiction creation, six miles south of the town, would doubtfully have gained the approbation of her 'genteel' ladies, to

whom artificial satellites, radio signals and far-distant galaxies would have been an undreamed-of horror! Chester, the county town, skirted by the meandering River Dee, is an ancient walled city of Roman origin, with a wealth of historic interest. Probably its most famous feature is The Rows, which consists of galleried streets of shops, reached by stairways; a feature that is quite unique. There is also what is believed to be the last surviving example of a sedan-chair, at the odd-sounding address of No. 13 City Walls. Cheshire, however, also has its own industrial areas, particularly those connected with the textile industry, as well as a salt mine at Winsford – proof that not all of this valuable mineral is of Siberian extraction.

Between the estuaries of the Rivers Mersey and Dee lies the Wirral Peninsula, the heart of the Merseyside playground, where miles of sand-dune-edged beaches are connected to the industrialised hub of Birkenhead by wharves and docks. Conjoined to this important flour-milling and shipbuilding centre by two tunnels under the Mersey, is the 13th-century fishing village that grew phenomenally during the Industrial Revolution – Liverpool – Europe's greatest Atlantic seaport. From the seven-mile stretch of densely-packed dockland along its waterfront rises the idiosyncratic outline of the celebrated Liver Building, its two main towers topped by mythical 'Liver' birds, after which the city is said to have been named. This cosmopolitan city also boasts two cathedrals, each of distinct, ecclesiastical architecture: Sir Giles Gilbert Scott's Gothic-inspired Anglican Cathedral and Sir Frederick Gibberd's contemporary Roman Catholic Metropolitan Cathedral, with its huge, conical 'lantern'.

Until the re-organisation of the county boundaries in 1974, Manchester, built by Agricola's legions on the banks of the Irwell River, was the mighty commercial hub of Lancashire, a 14th-century county palatine, bordered by the wild Pennine Moors on its eastern flank and by fertile lowlands to the west, against the Irish Sea. It is along this coastline, a popular resort area since the mid-18th century, that is sited the North West's busiest and most famous holiday centre of Blackpool, dominated by its 518 ft tower that oversees the six-mile long promenade, noted for its spectacular autumn illuminations. Off-shore lies one of the smallest independent sovereign countries under the crown, the tiny Isle of Man, its picturesque scenery and exceptionally mild climate providing ideal conditions for holiday activities. Douglas, the island's capital, is the home of the Tynwald, the Manx Parliament of Scandinavian origins that are earlier than those of Westminster.

Harnessed to the vast conurbation of Greater Manchester, and its fan of industrial centres that include the major cotton-spinning towns of Bolton and Oldham, Manchester's importance as a key cotton centre was firmly rooted during the 18th century, although Flemish weavers had established the weaving tradition over four hundred years earlier. This inland city became one of the country's largest seaports, handling the export of raw cotton and importing finished textiles, with the construction of the 35½-mile-long Manchester Ship Canal, which was opened in 1894. Although ravaged by the effects of the Industrial Revolution and by bomb damage during the Second World War, the city's extensive redevelopment schemes have already greatly altered and enhanced its visual image, but its crowning glory, however, is still the magnificent 15th-century Perpendicular Gothic Cathedral, its soaring, 280 ft tower containing a carillon of 23 bells.

Lake-strewn valleys amid craggy mountains, fern-covered hillsides and forested woodlands, tumbling waterfalls and carpets of wild flowers; little wonder that the spectacular scenery of Cumbria's Lake District inspired the celebrated 'Lake Poets' – Wordsworth, Southey and Coleridge – and a host of writers such as Beatrix Potter, who wrote and illustrated some of her charming children's books at Hill Top Farm in the village of Sawrey. Painters and photographers, sportsmen and ramblers, and, of course, mountaineers, who challenge the forbidding massifs that include Skiddaw, Helvellyn and England's second highest peak, Scafell, have also long been attracted to the Lakeland region, where, it is claimed, the sport of rock-climbing originated. The two largest lakes, Ullswater and Windermere are set amid a landscape that has remained virtually unchanged since Wordsworth first saw his 'host of golden daffodils', while the Tarns, near Coniston, is considered by many to be the prettiest of all the area's lakes. Yet Cumbria does not consist solely of Lakeland, as unquestionable as its beauty is. The Border region beyond Carlisle is rich in historical associations and remains. Here stand the fragments of the northern limit of the Roman Empire – Hadrian's Wall – and a wealth of prehistoric sites and castles, like the Border fortress of Carlisle Castle. Notable industrial centres include those of Whitehaven and Workington, while the Cumbrian coast, site of the Calder Hall atomic power station, reveals long stretches of sandy beaches, that, coupled with beautiful inland countryside, remain quite unspoiled for the enjoyment of all.

North East England: Humberside, North, West, and South Yorkshire, Cleveland, Durham, Tyne & Wear, Northumberland

'There is a spot, 'mid barren hills
Where Winter howls and driving rain,
But, if the dreary tempest chills,
There is a light that warms again.'

Emily Brontë

Once a part of the vast Anglo-Saxon kingdom of Northumbria, ruled at its inception by Aethelfrith during the early 7th century, the North East counties have been bound not only by their associated historical links but also by their common, natural resources of coal and iron-ore that contributed significantly to the industrial development initiated during the 18th century. Their rugged landscapes, too, from the wild, wind-blown Pennine Moors stretching northwards towards the Cheviot Hills, to their river-drained valleys, have much in common. Its history is possibly the most turbulent of England's regions, and it was not until after the Acts of Union – legislation uniting the Crowns of England and Scotland – in 1707, that the region began to develop its true potential. The boundaries of the three original counties of Yorkshire, Durham and Northumberland were effectively reorganised in 1974 and now comprise the above-listed seven counties; yet governmental demarcation lines cannot blot out their inextricable ties, forged by a shared experience throughout eons of time.

Centred around the Humber Estuary, the county of Humberside comprises most of the old East Riding of Yorkshire, plus the area around Goole. It was along the chalk-cliffed coastline where the Yorkshire Wolds terminate in the rocky promontory of Flamborough Head, just beyond the popular sea-side resort of Bridlington, that the Vikings successfully swept ashore in the 10th century – their once-victorious cries now echoed by the high-pitched shrieks of thousands of seabirds which today inhabit the striking northern cliffs. Officially Kingston-upon-Hull, Hull, lying on the broad Humber River and one of the country's leading sea-ports, is renowned for its great fishing fleets which have justly earned their reputation of landing a greater quantity of fish than any other British port. The city is also remembered as the native town of the dedicated anti-slavery campaigner William Wilberforce, whose home is now a museum. Of the county's many fascinating towns and villages, however, the most splendid is undoubtedly Beverley, with its glorious, twin-towered Gothic Minster, a flourishing market town since the Middle Ages, and the birthplace of the late-mediaeval martyr Bishop John Fisher.

Formed mainly from the former North Riding, the diverse landscape of North Yorkshire, littered with the remains of man from time immemorial, encompasses the wild, bleak North York Moors that rise beyond the Vale of Pickering, bordering the Yorkshire Wolds, and the broad expanse of the fertile Vale of York which is flanked to the west by the spectacular scenery of the Yorkshire Dales as they merge with England's spiny backbone, the Pennine Chain. In a region crammed with so many historical relics, it is difficult to do other than just pluck at random some of its bright jewels: close to Malton stands one of England's most palatial mansions in a perfectly matched setting, that of Castle Howard, created for the 3rd Earl of Carlisle by Sir John Vanbrugh, between 1699 and 1726; by the Wharfe River tower the splendid ruined remains of twelfth-century Bolton Abbey, and near Helmsley, above the River Rye, is sited one of the country's earliest Cistercian houses, magnificent Rievaulx Abbey, its ruined splendour seen to perfection against a densely-wooded backdrop. Popular sea-side resorts, such as Scarborough and Whitby, dot its coastline; dignified towns, like the fashionable inland spa of Harrogate, which is also a noted conference centre, add to its lustre, whilst a host of picturesque villages are scattered across its length and breadth. As if this were not enough, proud Yorkshiremen can also boast of their ancient Roman garrison-town of Eboracum – glorious York – much of its 2,000 years of history still vividly tangible inside the city walls. Its present name is derived from Jorvik, so called by the invading Danes who captured the city during the 9th century. Of all its treasures, however, pride of place must go to its breathtaking Minster, 'a poem of stone' that took over two and a half centuries to complete, between 1220 and 1470.

Famed for its woollen industry, centred on the important trading communities that include Bradford, Leeds and Halifax, which grew phenomenally during the Industrial Revolution as the old cottage industries moved closer to the coalfields and their valuable source of fuel, the West Yorkshire Moors, penetrated by the Aire and Calder rivers, have long supported the white-fleeced sheep that have grazed on the moorland for centuries past. It was this same bleak moorland turf that was trod by the famous Brontë family – Emily, Charlotte, Anne and Branwell, who lived in the romantic Old Parsonage at Haworth, a square, sandstone house that has been the Brontë Museum since 1928.

Below the moors the industrial heart of Yorkshire is contained within the metropolitan county of South Yorkshire. This largely industrialised region, especially in the Don Valley, is renowned for its iron and steel manufacture. Sheffield, set in an amphitheatre of the South Pennine slopes, is synonymous with the steel and cutlery industry, for the city has produced knife blades here for almost seven centuries.

Rugged and tempered like the stalwart people who laid not only their endeavour but also their landscape at the feet of progress during the Industrial Revolution, the counties of Cleveland, Durham and Tyne & Wear still bear, inevitably, the symbols that mark the region's industrial greatness. Yet it would be erroneous to suppose that the counties consist solely of the features of ship-building, iron, steel and chemical industries, for they too have their share of beauty, and nowhere is this more apparent than in the splendid cathedral city of Durham, built round a loop in the River Wear; its magnificent Norman Cathedral a shrine of St Cuthbert and also containing the tomb of the Venerable Bede within its richly ornamented interior. Along the coastline picturesque resorts boast long stretches of sandy beaches, while some of the finest scenery of the Pennine Chain is evident on the west Durham Moors.

Rich in history, England's most northerly county of Northumberland, bounded on the north by Scotland across the River Tweed and the Cheviot Hills, and flanked to the east by the North Sea, contains one of the most famous of all Roman remains – the spectacular relic of Hadrian's Wall which slices across the county from Haltwhistle to Wallsend in Tyne & Wear. Today, the tranquil farmland, south of the River Tweed, belies the savagery of the fierce Border Clashes – vividly evoked by the area's many ancient fortresses – perhaps the bloodiest that of Flodden Field where, in 1513, the blood of James IV and thousands of Scots and Englishmen was spilled on the earth now covered by tall ears of corn that flutter gently in the breeze. At Berwick-upon-Tweed, England's northernmost town, which was once a great Scottish port, stands an impressive stone bridge, of 17th-century origin, with no less than 15 arches; built by order of James I to connect the town of Tweedmouth on the opposite side of the estuary.

In any book on a country, however wide the coverage or strong the intent, a vast amount is inevitably omitted. It would be foolish to suppose that these pages only record the best that is to be seen and that there is little else worth showing. At best a book such as this can only serve to awaken an interest in objects and places that the reader may not be aware of, or to tinge with nostalgia that with which the reader is familiar, and in so doing to present just a few of the riches with which this country is so liberally endowed.

Washed by white-crested breakers, Godrevy Island Lighthouse right stands sentinel in the Cornish Bay of St Ives.

Cornwall, with its famous granite mass, Land's End, tumbling into the sea at the end of the Penwith Peninsula *previous page*, is steeped in the vestiges of history and legend: the stone ramparts of a 13th-century castle remain at Launceston *below*; according to legend St Michael's Mount *above* is part of the lost kingdom of Lyonesse, where once King Arthur's knights rode, and Tintagel Castle *left* stands on the site of what was one of his castles. Gwithian's Lighthouse appears on the horizon *right* beyond Gwithian's Sands, and on a Treen cliff *overleaf*, 'logan' rock, weighing about 65 tons, 'logs' or rocks, at the slightest touch.

The mile-long beach at Seaton, Devon above, sweeps from high cliffs in the west to the mouth of the Axe in the east. Torquay, in its superb panoramic setting overlooking Tor Bay below, is the largest and most famous of the Devonshire seaside resorts, and today Kingswear left is closely linked to it by ferries across the River Dart.

Characteristic of Cornwall's resorts, with their distinctive fishing village atmosphere, are: St Ives above right which sprang up around a small chapel built by St Ita in the 6th century; East Looe, seen from West Looe right, where pretty houses cluster in tiers around its ancient harbour, and Polperro overleaf strung along a narrow combe.

Sidmouth above right, *at the mouth of the River Sid, is a particularly attractive town with a pebble and shingle beach bordered by spectacular cliffs.*

Widecombe-in-the-Moor above lies as its name suggests high up on Dartmoor. Its church, which dates from c. 1500, has a high, pinnacled tower introduced by tin-miners keen to manifest their newly acquired wealth.

Thatched roofs are a characteristic part of the charm of Devonshire villages such as Buckland-in-the-Moor left, Bucks Mills below and Cockington, a well-known local showpiece right.

Magnificent stained glass windows adorn the east end of the Chapel of Our Lady *left* in Exeter Cathedral – possibly the greatest glory of one of the most historic cities of England.

Bath, in Somerset, which began in AD 44 as an important Roman settlement, is also a city of great historical interest. At its heart stands the superb 16th-century Abbey Church of St Peter and St Paul. In late-Perpendicular Gothic style, the abbey, with its glorious West Front *above* and intricate lectern *below*, is noted for its beautiful windows *right*.

Wells above and left, in Somerset, is particularly famous for its cathedral, begun in the 12th century. Its West Front below, originally embellished with nearly 400 statues of saints, angels and prophets, is one of the finest in Britain.

Only fragments remain of Glastonbury's 13th-century abbey above left and right, the last of a series on this site. Legend tells how Joseph of Arimathea came here to convert the English. As he leant on his staff to pray, it took root, indicating that the saint should stay and found a religious house.

Bath was made a show-piece for 18th-century architecture by architects such as John Wood the Younger who was responsible for the Royal Crescent right, an elegant, open design of thirty houses in a sweeping semi-ellipse, and by Robert Adam who designed the Florentine, shop-lined Pulteney Bridge left.

A graceful, 19th-century spire rising 285 feet from the ground rests on the fine 13th-century tower of St Mary Redcliffe in Bristol below.

The Clifton Suspension Bridge above, built by Brunel in 1864, spans the River Avon at a point where it flows between steep, limestone cliffs.

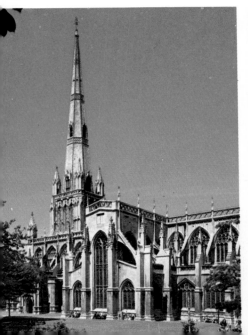

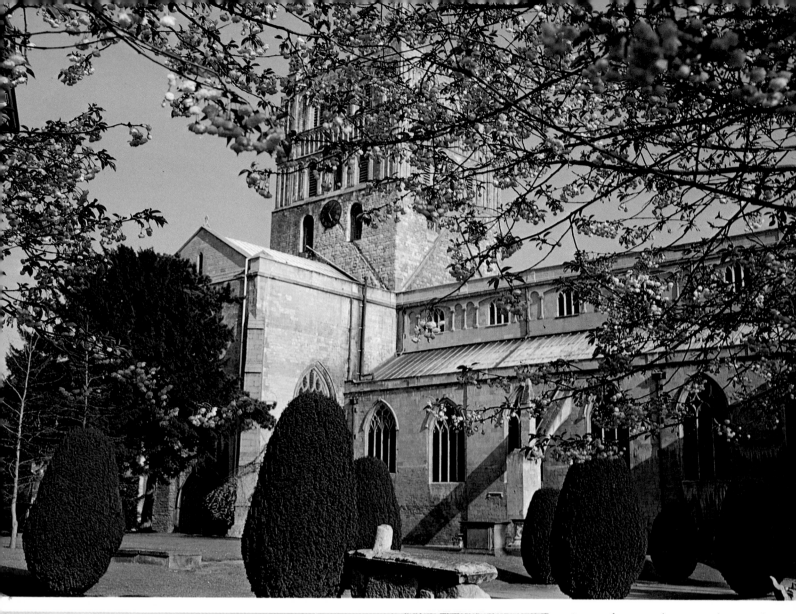

Among the many charming Gloucestershire villages with their distinctive stone houses which nestle amid leafy greenery, are Naunton above right and overleaf, Buckland below, and Dursley left. It was Bibury right, however, that William Morris described as 'the most beautiful village in England'.

Tewkesbury, the site of a Yorkist victory in the Wars of the Roses, contains a wealth of ancient houses and timbered inns. Its majestic abbey above is topped by a fine 132ft-high Norman tower, from the top of which can be seen panoramic views of the surrounding countryside.

St John's Lock at Lechlade *left* is just one of the many tranquil corners of Gloucestershire, where mellow Cotswold villages, such as Chipping Camden, with its impressive, mainly 15th-century church *centre right*, nestle amid the hills. Old, honey-coloured stone buildings *above* reveal the charm of Broadway, a lovely Worcestershire village which was known as 'The Painted Lady of the Cotswolds'. Also in Worcestershire, Pershore Abbey *below* and seen *bottom right* with St Andrew's Church, is noted for its superb, early-14th-century lantern tower, whilst at Overbury can be seen the fine, greatly restored church *top right*.

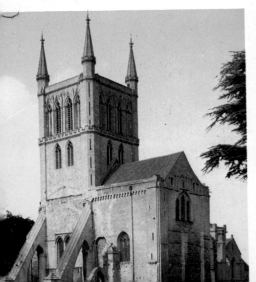

Pretty, thatched cottages, set in delightful flower-filled gardens above and below left, are part of the charm of Herefordshire, the 'land of the cider apple', a county which is noted for its wealth of outstandingly beautiful, small market towns. Ledbury, the birthplace of John Masefield, is a typical example, its cobbled Church Lane, lined with half-timbered buildings above, connecting the Market Place and the church. One of Herefordshire's most famous beauty spots is magnificent Symond's Yat where the meandering Wye River overleaf flows in its narrow gorge in a 5-mile loop around Huntsham Hill.

Holland House bottom right is set in the charming Worcestershire village of Cropthorne between Pershore and Evesham. An important market town at the heart of the Vale of Evesham, Evesham has retained the ruins of its ancient abbey with a fine, Perpendicular bell tower below and a half-timbered gateway on an original Norman stone base centre right.

The old water mill above right completes the setting of picturesque Tudor houses at Tewkesbury in Gloucestershire.

Rising from the Wiltshire plain, the vast monoliths of Stonehenge right, completed c. 1250 BC, and the brooding Avebury Stone Circle above, c. 1800 BC, remain shrouded in mystery – for, although it would seem that they had some religious significance, the reason for their construction is still a complete enigma.

Cut into the hillside near Weymouth, the huge figure of the Osmington man (also known as King George III) left rides his gigantic horse, whilst from the 'water meadows' of the Avon rises the 404ft. spire of Salisbury Cathedral below.

Sheltered by Ballad Down, the chalk spires of Old Harry Rocks above jut from the sea close to the Dorset resort of Swanage, and further along the coast, a lighthouse below warns of potentially hazardous rocks at renowned Portland Bill. Spectacular Durdle Door left and top right, a headland out of which the sea has carved a huge 'door', divides two wide bays beneath the sheer, chalk cliffs, and like Man o' War Bay bottom right reveals the unequivocal grandeur of the Dorset coast at Lulworth, whilst beyond the tiled roofs of Corfe Castle centre right rise the splendid ruined remains of a fortress which dates from the time of William the Conqueror to the 14th century.

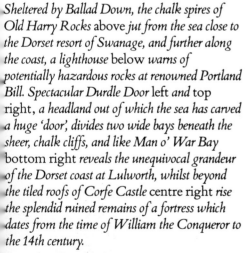

Immortalised in the novels of Thomas Hardy, the county of Dorset is noted for its rolling downlands, tranquil countryside and picturesque thatched dwellings, such as Three Airs Cottage above, as well as its delightful seaside resorts.

Situated on Poole Bay, Bournemouth, with its superb golden sands left and top left, is among the county's most famous resorts. Lush fields roll away to charming Swanage above right, its sandy beach and cliff-lined coast providing a perfect setting for the holidaymaker, whilst Weymouth below right, a packet station for the Channel Islands, was popularised by George III. Named after the Augustinian priory church Holy Trinity, Christchurch bottom left is also a popular holiday centre, at the confluence of the Avon and Stour rivers.

In the minster of the pretty town of Wimborne Minster below is contained the tomb of Ethelred I who was slain nearby in a Danish battle during the 9th century.

...astings in Sussex, with its picturesque Sinnock ...uare above, has preserved much of its ...aracter as a fishing port and original member of ...e Cinque ports, whilst the ancient town of ...ewes, which rose to prominence after the ...orman Conquest, contains a wealth of historic ...terest in its steep and narrow, cobbled streets ...low.

Bodiam Castle left and centre right is a ...agnificent fortress built in 1386 to discourage ...rench raiders from sailing up the River Rother, ...d further up the same river lies Fittleworth, ...ith its Old Mill bottom right decked with the ...sset and green of trailing creepers.

The Normans built the original Arundel ...astle to defend the valley of the Arun River ...gainst raiders, and its successor still dominates ...e valley top right.

In 1843 the Duke of Devonshire inherited a small village on the south coast and set out to create from it a rival to the nearby Sussex town of Brighton. The result was Eastbourne above and right, a watering-place which was popular in the 19th century and which has remained so to this day. To the west of the town stands Beachy Head lighthouse below backed by soaring chalk cliffs rising 600ft above the waters of the English Channel, and Newhaven left, which is a busy cross-Channel port.

Rye *right* and *bottom left was* once a hill fort with formidable ramparts almost ringed by the sea. The sea receded in the late-16th century, but the town has never lost its character and individuality. The steep cobbled street *above*, leading to the old Mermaid Inn *top left which* opened in 1420, recalls the days when Rye was an important port.

East Grinstead *centre left has* preserved its market town atmosphere, and, in the heart of Brighton, the Lanes *below* are the surviving streets of the original fishing hamlet.

Canterbury in Kent, an ancient city with more than 2,000 years of history, is dominated by its magnificent cathedral *overleaf*. Dating from Norman times, this historic place of pilgrimage is the Mother Church of Anglicans throughout the world.

In Tenterden, weatherboarded houses below line the streets of this Kentish market town which in the 15th century was made a member of the Cinque Port of Rye, the town at that period lying only 2 miles from the sea. It is also reputed to be the birthplace of William Caxton, the father of English printing.

One of the county's prettiest villages is undoubtedly that of Chilham with its Tudor and Jacobean houses bottom right, whilst the marketplace of Faversham centre right is also surrounded by picturesque buildings, most of which date from Tudor or Stuart times. Half-timbered cottages overlook the West Gate gardens in Canterbury top right, and in Royal Tunbridge Wells left and above, the Pantiles, an 18th-century shopping walk shaded by lime trees, has changed little since the town was in its prime as an elegant Regency spa.

Familiar red London buses cross *Lambeth Bridge* above *against a background of the old London skyline.*

Epitomising the new London is the futuristic silhouette of the *Post Office Tower* top left which houses, in addition to a great deal of technological hardware, a revolving restaurant.

Probably one of the most familiar views of London by night is *Piccadilly Circus* centre left, with its famous neon signs.

A festive touch is added to *Trafalgar Square* and its beautiful fountains by the erection of an illuminated *Christmas tree* bottom left, *an annual gift from the people of Norway,* and to *Regent Street* below, by gaily-coloured decorations suspended far above the heads of Christmas shoppers.

The imposing clock tower of Big Ben stands as a symbol of London above the night-time traffic in *Whitehall* right.

Dominating the broad-ribboned Thames below right, *Windsor Castle, in Berkshire, is a favourite home of the Royal Family and the largest castle in England, covering 13 acres. Founded by William the Conqueror on the site of an earlier stronghold, the castle is divided into three parts: the Lower Ward, which includes the Curfew Tower centre left, and St George's Chapel; the Middle Ward, with the imposing Round Tower topped by a lofty flagpole above right, and the Upper Ward, containing the State Apartments. To the north of the Round Tower is the 14th-century gate above, known as the Norman gate.*

The castle itself is still the scene of colourful processions such as that of the Garter Ceremony top and bottom left, attended by Her Majesty the Queen, and Windsor is also the venue each spring of the Royal Windsor Horse Show below.

The Royal River Thames has a gentle and very English beauty as it passes towns and villages such as Abingdon below, one of the oldest and most important towns in Berkshire, and picturesque Molesey, in Surrey left.

It is also the historic river which borders the grounds of Hampton Court above, the splendid palace begun in 1514 by Cardinal Wolsey and acquired by Henry VIII when Wolsey fell in disgrace. Among a wealth of features is Anne Boleyn's Gateway right, surmounted by a magnificent astronomical clock made for the King, and a superb example of Tudor brickwork Five of Henry's wives lived at the palace, and the ghosts of Jane Seymour and Catherine Howard are said to roam its corridors.

Like cricket centre right, *punting on the River Isis* top right *is a traditional summer recreation. The Romans called the Thames at Oxford the Isis. Exactly where the Thames becomes the Isis and vice versa is not clearly defined but the river flows through this great seat of learning as it does through the pretty 'Home County' towns of Whitchurch* left, *Goring Lock* below *and Wallingford Lock* bottom right. *At Henley* above *it makes another claim to fame; in 1839 the world's first river regatta was held here and the tradition still persists.*

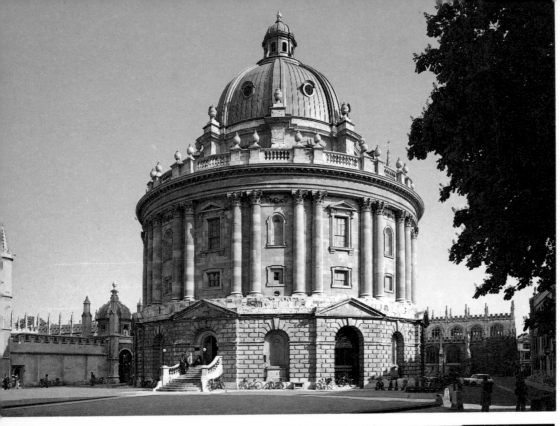

The university town of Oxford, renowned as a great seat of learning, is also noted for its magnificent architecture which continues the tradition of Matthew Arnold's 'Beautiful city! . . . whispering from her towers the last enchantments of the Middle Age . . .'.

Designed by Sir Christopher Wren in 1644 in the style of a Roman theatre, the Sheldonian Theatre bottom left is now used for university functions such as degree ceremonies.

The Bodleian Library below, which dates from 1480 and now holds over 2½ million books, is one of the world's most important libraries, and the neighbouring Radcliffe Camera top left, designed by James Gibbs in 1737, is one of the university reading rooms, holding 600,000 books in its underground store.

The quadrangles left and above right are those of Oriel College and St Edmund Hall, and the façade below right is part of St John's College, founded in 1555, whilst beyond the college rooftops above rises the soaring spire of St Mary the Virgin, the university church which is the third church to stand on the site.

The gentle undulating county of Suffolk, with its picturesque villages such as Sapiston above, is closely associated with John Constable, who was born in the county in 1776. The artist was at school in Lavenham right, the most resplendent of Suffolk wool towns, with fine, mediaeval timber houses. The market square is dominated by the Guildhall top left, which at various times has been a prison, a workhouse and an almshouse. Built shortly after the founding of the Guild of Corpus Christi in 1529, one of its corner posts carries a full-length figure of the 15th Lord de Vere, founder of the Guild. Also of note is the original Wool Hall which has been incorporated in the Swan Hotel bottom left.

Typical of Suffolk's rural charm is Cavendish centre left, the former ancestral village of the Dukes of Devonshire, where colour-washed and thatched cottages and familiar church steeple cluster around the village green.

Kersey below is one of the prettiest villages. Here the street of dark-timbered houses runs through a watersplash where ducks still take precedence over cars.

Norfolk is perhaps best known for its Broads, open expanses of water with navigable approach channels seen left and below with the county's familiar windmills. Together with rivers and man-made waterways they form about 200 miles for boating, and villages like Potter Heigham above are ever ready to provide for holidaymakers.

At Castle Acre above right are the ragged remains of the Cluniac priory, founded by William de Warenne, son-in-law of William the Conqueror, whilst Blickling Hall right, begun in 1616, was at one time owned by the Boleyn family.

Cambridge, on the banks of the River Cam, a flourishing commercial centre in the Middle Ages, is renowned for its university which was established as long ago as the early 13th century.

Queen's College top left was founded no less than three times in the course of the 15th century, while Trinity Hall below was, remarkably, founded only once – in 1350 by the Bishop of Norwich. It is the only college still known as a Hall to distinguish it from Trinity College, the lovely bridge of which, over the River Cam, can be seen above. The 'Bridge of Sighs' right links two of the buildings of St John's College, founded by the mother of Henry VII in 1511. Possibly the greatest glory of Cambridge, however, is King's College Chapel bottom left, considered by some to be the finest Gothic building in Europe.

Yet Cambridge does not hold a monopoly on the county's fine architecture. The splendid landmark of Ely Cathedral centre left, dating back to the 11th century, is a triumph of mediaeval architecture; its superb octagonal lantern created by Alan de Walsingham to replace an earlier tower which collapsed in 1322.

Despite the industrial development of the northern part of the county, Warwickshire still has its 'leafy lanes' dotted with attractive villages like Barton on the Heath below and with imposing country homes. Packwood House above is a lovely example of a timber-framed Tudor building, with later 17th-century additions, which was begun in 1556 by William Fetherston. Its 17th-century garden of yew trees left is a symbolic representation of the Sermon on the Mount. Compton Wynyates right is another superb example of Tudor architecture and here, too, the stone and weathered brick are offset by yews and hedges tailored into neat, formal shapes.

The old market town of Stratford-upon-Avon, birthplace of William Shakespeare, has become one of the world's foremost tourist attractions. Among a wealth of historic monuments, one of the most charming is Anne Hathaway's Cottage *above* and *right*, *the thatched and timbered house in which Shakespeare's wife was born, situated one mile west of the town at Shottery.* Overlooking the River Avon, the Royal Shakespeare Theatre can be seen *below,* and *left the beautiful parish church of Holy Trinity, Shakespeare's burial place.*

Unique galleried shops have been preserved in the heart of Chester, Cheshire, overleaf.

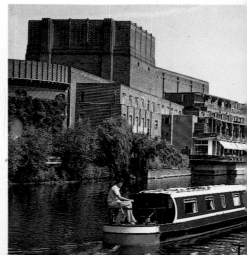

Liverpool's famous dockside frontage *above and left*, dominated by the twin towers of the Royal Liver Building which is surmounted by the legendary 'Liver' birds, extends for seven miles along the Mersey estuary. In the midst of the busy metropolis, Seeton Park *above right* provides a welcome retreat, whilst in its own quiet setting stands the Anglican Cathedral *right*, begun in 1904 by Sir Giles Gilbert Scott.

The 15th-century Perpendicular Gothic cathedral, the interior of which is shown *below*, is one of the showpieces of Manchester.

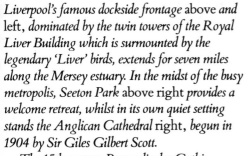

It was Grasmere's setting, below Helm Crag and Nab Scar and above Grasmere Lake, which caused Wordsworth to pronounce the village above 'the loveliest spot that man hath ever found', but the description could be applied to any number of beauty spots in Cumbria – Crummock Water above left, *a lovely 2½-mile long lake to the north-west of Buttermere;* tranquil Elterwater left, *at the entrance to the Langdale valleys, and picturesque Borrowdale* below, *close to magnificent Derwent Water* right, *at 1¼ miles across, the widest of the Lakeland Lakes.*

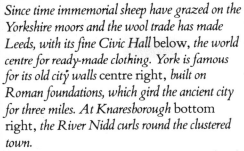

Since time immemorial sheep have grazed on the Yorkshire moors and the wool trade has made Leeds, with its fine Civic Hall *below, the world centre for ready-made clothing. York is famous for its old city walls* centre right, *built on Roman foundations, which gird the ancient city for three miles. At Knaresborough* bottom right, *the River Nidd curls round the clustered town.*

The North Yorkshire coast is punctuated with fishing ports and seaside towns such as Whitby left, *dominated by the jagged sandstone ruins of the Abbey* above, *founded in the 7th century, and Robin Hood's Bay* top right, *a pretty fishing village where red-roofed cottages jostle for space along the sea front.*

Yorkshire is rich in ecclesiastical architecture, and York is second only to Norwich in the number of old churches included within its limits. In Museum Gardens stand the ruins of the 13th-century St Mary's Abbey *above*, but the city's glorious Minster *left* is undoubtedly York's greatest pride – famed for its West Front and towers and a wealth of splendid mediaeval stained glass.

Made famous by Landseer's painting 'Bolton Abbey in Olden Times', the Abbey at Bolton *below*, by the banks of the River Wharfe, was founded in the early 12th century. The site of Rievaulx Abbey *below right*, one of the earliest Cistercian buildings in England, was granted by Walter L'Espec to a group of Cistercian monks in 1131, and the impressive ruins of Whitby Abbey *centre right* date from the 13th century.

Durham Cathedral above, standing on a 70ft rock surrounded on three sides by the River Wear, was begun in 1093 by the Norman Bishop, William of Calais. Older still is the enormous stone pile of Bamburgh Castle below and overleaf, once the seat of the first kings of Northumbria, and just off the Northumberland coast, on Holy Island right, stands the small, 16th-century castle of Lindisfarne.

The product of more recent engineering, the New Tyne Bridge left is one of the five bridges spanning the Tyne at Newcastle.